I Will Never Be Number One in His

Life:

The Story of Dating Down Low Men

Volume I

Cordaro Dont'e Santiago

I Will Never Be Number One in His Life: The Story of Dating
Downlow Men Vol 1

ISBN # 978-1535311885

Dedication

I would like to dedicate this body of work, to my Grandmother....Big Ma. You were my light and my inspiration my entire life. When you were alive, I felt like I was King of the World. Then, one day you were gone. My world fell completely apart. I went through so much without your loving guidance, and I didn't think I would make it through to the end. This book is a reflection of all my mistakes and all my success after your death. I wish you were here to help me celebrate, but I know you are smiling down on me from heaven.

Love you Grandma!

~Cordaro Dont'e Santiago

Acknowledgements

To My Family and Friends

Thank you for loving me and not loving me - they both made me who I am today. No regrets...We ALL have come a long way. We can only go up from here!

~Cordaro Dont'e Santiago

To My Mother

Words cannot express how much I love you! You are and always will be my Mother. You may have not always been perfect, but you always did the best you could. I now understand the power your addiction had over you, and I no longer blame you - or myself for that. I am grateful you are still in my life and we will shine from here on out together.

~Cordaro Dont'e Santiago

To My Father

I've tried my entire childhood and early teen years to connect with you. I never gave up hope that we would become closer. Then I became a man...in ways that I wish I had a Father to turn to. I don't blame you for the choices I made - I thank you for showing me the kind of Father I never want to be..... I love you Dad

To My Editor

Batch, you came all the way through for me!!! Thank you so much for all your time and effort. Can't wait to celebrate the success of this book with you! You are truly my Batch for Life!

~Cordaro Dont'e Santiago

To The Down Low Men

You are the reason I wrote this book in the first place. I have made so many mistakes by opening my heart to men like you… I hope this book will one day open your eyes soon, and realize there is no point in hiding who you really are. BE FREE!

~Cordaro Dont'e Santiago

Foreword

"Only the human mind invents categories and tries to force facts into separated pigeon-holes. The living world is a continuum in each and every one of its aspects. The sooner we learn this concerning sexual behavior the sooner we shall reach a sound understanding of the realities of sex." ~~Alfred Kinsey

This book was birthed from a *WORLD OF HURT!* I began writing every single thought, emotion *(whether good or bad)* I was feeling, and before you knew it - I had a book! My goal is that this book will help the next young boy, struggling with his sexuality and his tormented home life; to finally feel brave enough to just BE! I have been through SO much in my life, and these events shaped who I am today. I know there are young boys, teenagers, young men - out there who have been, and are going through some of the same things I have been through. Read this book with your whole heart, and you will be set free!

Table of Contents

Prologue

"If I fail, if I succeed

At least I'll live as I believe

No matter what they take from me

They can't take away my dignity

Because the greatest love of all

Is happening to me

I found the greatest love of all

Inside of me

"I decided long ago, never to walk in anyone's shadows

Whitney Houston, "The Greatest Love of All"

~

To this day I still have not discovered this kind of love for myself. For as long as I can remember, I never really learned how to love myself.

I don't think I ever knew how.

Growing up with my mother, who would have a new man every week, and my grandmother who tried to buy my affection; it was impossible to learn how to love myself. No one around me was showing me the proper way to love. My father was only in the picture when he was high or drunk, and beating on my mother. She was always waiting with open arms every time to take him back. Originally, I thought my attraction and passion for men was birthed out of a need for affection - because I wasn't shown any growing up. Later, the attraction would become sexual. I was overweight, which didn't help my self-esteem, and many guys weren't interested in me because of my weight. So I felt like I had to make them love me, in order to help me love myself. I would give them money, and trade sexual favors, in an effort to keep them around. When a guy would call my phone, *(for whatever reason)* that was enough to make me feel *"hot"* in my eyes. I'll call the first person who took advantage of me in this way the ***"home invader"***. We would all be devastated, to come home, and find that we had been robbed of all our belongings; which we worked so hard for. This is how my heart felt every time he would leave me.

"There is no medicine

To cure this pain of mine,

I'm tired and emotionally drained.

The knife's edge pierced my heart.

The moment I knew,

You were lying,

That's when things fell apart.

You told me,

I was Bonnie to your Clyde,

But when your friends were around,

You wanted to deny my love.

Why did I stress myself over a man?

Who didn't really love me?

I cried to make your world perfect,

But your perfection caused a disconnect…

Not from you,

But from me.

I put you on a pedestal,

Using my heart as a footstool.

And when I reached to grab your hand,

You pushed me in the pool,

Deep, drowning…

Knowing I don't like to swim.

Drowning…

Because I couldn't keep from crying.

You left me dying.

I ended up lying,

When people ask me,

How my weekend was going."

~Cordaro Santiago

Chapter I: I Get It from My Momma

We both exhale, he pushes off of me and kisses my ass cheeks as he gets up. I wipe the sweat from my face, as I pause with a frown upon my face. I just had one of the greatest sexual encounters of my life, and I can't even show excitement; because he was on the phone with his wife. When I say it was the greatest, I mean it! It was amazing. His tongue was so long, (when it was deep in my ass) that it gave me the chills. His dick had a nice curve to it, so when he would go deep inside me, I would have to take a deep breath. He rushed to the bathroom to avoid her hearing the television in the background. He was late coming home, so he was telling her he was stuck in traffic, and that he would stop to grab dinner. I climb out of bed, and walk behind him in the bathroom, as he smacks my ass. His wife asked; "what was that noise?" and he says; "I hit a pothole." So, I got down on my knees, and started sucking his dick, just to make him get off the phone. I succeeded. He ended up telling his wife, he had an incoming call from work, and he will call her back. Before hanging up, he told his daughter he loves her. He places the phone down as if, the conversation with his wife and child - meant nothing to him; and we go for round two. This is what I have to contend with, being involved with a man who likes both Men and Women; but chooses to hide it and only date women in the real world. By the way (that's the definition) of a Down Low Man (a man on the DL). I have gained an indepth understanding of down low men, and this is what prompted me to write this book.

Men who enjoy the idea of being in the presence of other men.

Men who enjoy having sexual encounters with other men.

Men who aren't ready to dive into the pool of outward moral judgment from the world with both feet.

Men who continue to lead their double lives in hopes that one day, not only will he accept the truth, but so will the world.

Let's be honest, the world will never accept it. In the eyes of a DLM, it is easier to live a double life, than to admit his true feelings. Who wants to be judged by the people they call family? The people you have looked up to your entire life? They hear you're **"gay"** and instantly look at you like you're a tourist from another country. They simply can't figure you out. Maybe this is how Jesus felt, when Judas betrayed him and watched the very people he loved crucify him. How can I expect a man to come out of the closet and tell his family and friends, ***"guess what gang, I am gay", when he can't even be honest with himself.*** I don't want to pressure him, but at the same time, I don't think I should suffer, simply because his world will change forever. It is fucking hard being a gay black man in America! Being gay in some people minds means we only want to have raw sex because no one takes relationships seriously in the gay community. For some reason gays do not believe we are going to be around long enough to have long relationships, so what's the point. Then some believe they don't deserve it because this was not the intention of God when he made man. Then we just have simple minded people who believe being gay is just a phase that people go through.

Now add all of that on top of being black in America and we are fucked. I already worry about having to put my hands in the air when an officer, that is supposed to protect and serve me, shoots me. I have to now understand that when I go into a gay club, the room may not be filled with happiness but someone full of hatred that may want to take my life. I'm sick of straight men feeling pressure from society, so if a gay man looks at him, his first instinct is to kill him. I am so surprised that the black gay man hasn't given up. Black men are supposed to be the provider for the family so he can't be a sissy right? Why are all the good looking men in jail, dead or gay? You can't be masculine and be gay at the same time right? How do you attend church and sing to the lord and suck dick at the same time? All of these questions are asked of a gay black man. It amazes me that in a city as diverse as Chicago, differences are still to be feared, not embraced. Walking through boystown, I have no qualms holding the hand of a date, but that behavior doesn't fly in the predominantly black neighborhood I grew up in. There, if I dare traverse the streets with another man—let alone a white man—the shit will hit the fan. My skin color may be the right shade, but my neighbors' perception of me makes the air thick with contempt. No man should be judged, especially one wearing good shoes.

I learned a lot from my mother. She taught me how to sing, dance, and ride a bike. She also taught me how to fall in and out of love. My mother couldn't stay in a stable relationship if she wanted to. My mother has always been a beautiful woman inside and outside. When she was younger, my mother was a great singer and dancer; and could very well have made a career in the arts out of it. My mother has always taken pride in her appearance and had to because of who her mother was. My mother was a socialite and had quite a few friends. If you wanted to have a good time, and a ton of laughs, my mother was and still is the one to call. I see so much of my mother in me and I love it. For the longest time, I thought the women in my family were cursed, because none of them had successful relationships. My grandmother divorced and remarried before I was born, and my second grandfather had a lot of mental and physical health issues. He died when I was four years old. My mother dated a lot of men after she and my father had me. I can remember at least six men that actually affected my life in some way. None of her relationships would end well, but that never stopped her from moving on to the next one. I always wondered why my mother was unsatisfied unless she had a man sleeping in her bed. She always seemed sad when she had to sleep alone. As a kid, I would try to make her smile, but no matter what I did; I couldn't fill that void in her heart. I thought the void was missing a man, when in truth the void came from her inability to love herself. I also had a cousin who was a little older than me. We were very close, and a lot of people thought we were brother and sister. Back then, she was someone I looked up to for inspiration and how to be sexy to attract a man's attention. She was extremely sexy and wasn't shy about showing it. If she ever dated a guy I knew he was going to be sexy as hell, and she would never disappoint. Her relationships didn't last long at all, because of her wandering eyes; but she always had the time of her life while she was dating.

I understood exactly what my mother was going through when it came to parental guidance. Granddaddy was never around, which is why my mother was always drawn to the attention of men. This cycle continued with me, because I felt the same way regarding my father. My mother came from a small family, but my father's family - the Johnson/Santiago family was large. Someone was always having a baby or a party. Everyone was always getting together for some kind of festivity. It must have seemed like the perfect location to drop me off, based on the fact it would always happen. My father thought leaving me at my grandmother's house to play meant he was spending quality time with me *(not a good idea...but I'll discuss that later.* He never took me to the park, to a movie, or to a baseball game. I can't even tell you important facts, or give you any important details about my father. It was so hard feeling like I shared genes with a stranger. A man who didn't know me, and I didn't know him. He says he knows me, but being a sperm donor, doesn't make you a parent. I mean who doesn't know their father's favorite movie, book, color, food, or pastime? **ME** that's who!

So, my mother began to search for love elsewhere and with other men.

So did I.

There was one point when I actually thought my mother found *"the one."* This guy worked with my mother and was at least eight years her junior. Thinking about him now, I remember he had so much swagger. *(I'm not sure what that slang would have been for the early 90's though, but damn he had it.)* He was calm and easy going, and looked like one of the members of *Boyz II Men*. I was happy for my mother, because I thought she had finally found love. This man did everything for her that my dad didn't do. He actually had a job, he was funny and he took my mother out all the time. He even treated me like his own son. Of course this wasn't pleasing to my father. What I failed to mention was, my dad had a really bad temper. I'd seen plenty of the bruises my mother tried to hide with makeup and a smile.... but she couldn't fool me.

My father wasn't ready to let her love another man. Which is typical in the African American household....actually, it's pretty typical in quite a few cultures. A man can cheat on a women all damn day long, but won't let her move on until he is ready for her to move on. Nine times out of ten, he is never ready for her to move on.

My father abused my mother so bad, it was hard to stomach at times. His mood, when he was sober was amazing. I have quite a few great memories of my dad making me and my mother laugh. I think laughter was the key to my mother's heart. She loved to smile, and any man that could do that; won her heart. My father seemed like a totally different person at times. How could a man make a women laugh, cry and be terrified all in the same day? My poor my mother tried her best to please him, (like she does everyone) but it was never enough. There were times I was afraid my dad was going to kill my mother. I never understood why he was so mad at her for moving on, when he cheated on her and had kids with another women while they were together. One time my mother and I were home watching the movie "Bringing down the House" waiting for my dad to show up. My mother was excited because it seemed like we could finally have a family

18

bonding moment. My mother ordered pizza and had some cold soda waiting on him to show up. Hours passed and I was getting very tired, so my mother started up the movie because I really wanted to see it and only thirty minutes into the movie there was a loud bang on our door. Even though we were watching a comedy, this bang freaked the hell out of the both of us. Then someone started yelling my mother's name, and we both knew it was my dad. Well honestly I didn't know who this person was, he sounded like my dad in his tone, but his delivery of calling upon my mother was not the dad I wanted to see. I could tell he was drunk because his words were slurred. I didn't want my mother to open the door because I had a feeling that something bad was going to happen if she let him in….

but she did

I can tell she was hesitant about letting him come in, but she opened the door and was greeted with a punch. The next noise I heard was my mother hitting the floor screaming at my father to get off of her. I jumped up yelling at my dad because I didn't want him hurting my mother anymore. I stood over him as he was choking my mother screaming at him to stop and the look in his eyes was of a monster.

That was not my dad looking at me

He finally let my mother go and he stormed out the door. My mother, being the amazing women she is, started crying, but not from the abuse, but because I just witnessed the worst behavior a man could give to a women - which changed the way I looked at my father for the rest of my life.

Needless to say, my dad did everything in his power to get rid of my mother's new man. It got so bad, my mother's new man planned to secretly kill my father in an alleyway one time. See my father thought this guy was a punk, but he wasn't. He was an ex drug dealer, who still had plenty of connections. He was respectful and told my mother what his plans were to get rid of my father. I couldn't blame him - my father burst the windows out of this man's car and constantly left him threatening voicemails. I actually didn't care what happened to my father. I mean I couldn't miss a man I barely even knew. I think my mother pondered the thought for a while, but she couldn't go through with it, so she stopped him and ended the relationship to keep everyone safe. I don't think I ever saw my mother cry as much as she did after that. Her heavy tears spilled over into her wine glass, and then landed on the coke pipe she smoked. I was sad as well. I lost the only real "father figure" I had in my life.

He was sexy as fuck...those lips.

The silhouette of his dick, as he got out of the shower…

Why did I feel this way about him?

I was only nine or ten years old, but now I realize that he was the first man I fell in love with. That was the moment I realized that maybe I liked men as more than father figures.

At times I thought I was the reason my parents couldn't make it work. Everyone keeps telling me even today, that my mother and father were attached to the hip love birds from the moment they laid eyes on each other, but I never once saw that interaction between them. All I saw was pain, abuse, anger and sadness. I do believe the only good thing my parents had in common was me, but I don't believe I was enough to save this horrific dark tale. My father ended up cheating on my mother and had two others kids while he was still in a very open relationship with my mother. When those kids came into the picture everything changed. I started to see how great of a father he was capable of being to my sisters, but I never received that same treatment. He adored my sisters, they were not dropped off at my grandmother's house when we were all together like I was.

I just didn't understand why he treated me like I wasn't apart of him.

The grass was not greener on the other side, because he was beating the hell out of my sisters' mother as well. I even think he beat her worse than my mother or maybe her bruises where easier to see because she was light skinned. With all of this chaos going on my mother still decided that it was the right idea to keep on taking my dad back anytime he wanted to show up. I don't understand why she did because the night always ended with her being bruised or with him threatening her if she had another man. I was just tired of my parents being unhappy.

I WAS THE PROBLEM

I wasn't sure how I could take myself out of the equation to make their life happier. I knew I had to do something the moment I found my mother trying to kill herself. The moment I had to sit on the side of the bed pumping prescription pills out of my mother's stomach was the moment I knew I had to be "dealt with". My mother cried all day from embarrassment. I'm not actually sure if she was crying because she was embarrassed or if she was upset that she was still alive. I decided to go to school still, but first I went into my room and looked in the mirror. I cried because when I looked at myself I saw nothing but hurt, anger, abuse and a useless soul looking back at me. I started to punch myself in the stomach and face because I just wanted it all to end.

I went to school and tried to hide my bruises, but it didn't work. I got called to the principal's office and was asked a lot of questions about my bruises. I thought about lying and saying that I was beaten up by a bully (which wouldn't be far from the truth or not believable), or saying that I fell down during a sports activity. Then I realized this was my way out.

THIS WAS MY WAY OF ALLOWING MY PARENTS TO BE HAPPY AGAIN!

So I decided to lie, but in a way it would benefit my parents. I told the principal that my parents would hit me from time to time and I that I was scared to go back home. All I wanted was for my parents to fall back in love, the love I was told existed before I was born. I had to remove myself from the picture regardless if I wouldn't see my family again. My principal was very familiar with my family and she didn't believe a word that came out of my mouth, so she called my mother to come and get me. I didn't realize how much my mother loved me until she realized how her addition to drugs and my father made me feel so unhappy and unwanted. My mother went to rehab to get her some well-deserved help and to focus on being a better mother to love and care for me and not worry about what a man needed from her. I needed my mother. My dad didn't change and wasn't going to. Instead of beating up my mother he just kept on beating up his current women until my mother got back home. My father never understood how his actions made me hate him more and more each day. He never stopped to take ownership of his actions and how his drinking, drugs and overall behavior made me not want to trust men. Actually, my father was the first man to never put me first in his life and I can't tell you how much that really hurt me. Now my father is suffering from having two of his legs removed because of his diabetes. I can't help but to think if this is the universe way of paying him back finally for all of those years of abuse my mother went through? I have yet to visit him, I mean it is hard for me to care for a stranger.

The last time I trusted you,
You left me out to dry in the sun.
I damn near drowned,
In a pool of my own blood,
Lying next to a loaded gun.
There were bullets left,
To be used.
Anger and abuse,
Anger because once again,
I trusted a fantasy,
A thought that life together,
Living in a beach house in the sand,
Was our destiny.
But I came to my senses,
Back to reality
And noticed the flame had gone away for eternity.

Now I know (hypothetically)

You're not the one for me.

Too little too late,

Got my ass whooped,

By misery and hate.

Abuse was the second bullet

You left for me

. You made me promises,

You were never going to keep.

Threw my dreams over a bridge

And acted like you never knew.

My dreams of music and acting weren't shit to you,

As long as that nut came out my job was through.

And you expect me to trust love again?

Fuck love….

Love left me on the side of the road,

Of success and happiness.

I tried to click my heels

But home is not where the heart is.

I don't trust love.

I will never use these bullets

Or take that shot

Chapter II: Stepfather Blues

At the tender age of eight years old, I began to notice that I had an attraction towards men. I was always staring at the guys in my gym class during our regular exercises at school. I really didn't have a lot of male friends in school. Mostly because of my size, my glasses and the way I carried myself. As a young boy, I was very feminine. I believed that women were respected and seen as sexual creatures, and that was how I wanted to be seen. I never thought my behavior was different. I didn't see anything wrong with 'sashaying' when I walked or talking sassy with my friends.

My mother never corrected me, so why would I want to stop?

I would play dress up in my mother's clothes, while she was at work or out running errands. I remember putting on her long robes, lipstick and nail polish; and acting out scenes from *Waiting to Exhale*, (especially the scene where Bernadine burned all her husband's shit). I would take all the clean clothes out the laundry bin, and throw them all around the house screaming lines from that scene. My mother caught me one day, and all she did was laugh; because she thought I was just acting. From that moment on, my mother and grandmother would have me act out various scenes from movies in front of their friends. I was always asked to act out the female characters, because I could do them so well. I loved the attention I received from it and that carried over into other aspects of my life.

There was a point when I realized I really needed some male attention:

The moment I started playing sports.

Before this, the only attention I received was from the bullies who picked on me or would beat me up every day. I started playing baseball during recess, and with the local park district. This was the closest I came to getting the male attention I craved without being considered gay. I enjoyed the hugs, the high fives and the fathers of the other players smiling at me. During recess at school, I was always the last person picked for the team, mainly because of my size. However, I was always a valuable player for the team. I started getting the respect that I always wanted from the guys at school. It was my way of getting the attention I wanted from guys. Sometimes I would find an excuse to accidentally touch one of my teammates.

Maybe rub up against their butts.

Or accidently touched their penises.

Since I was now in their inner circle, they no longer judged me when I would accidentally touched them. Everything seemed to be going well at the time. My itch was simply for light touch and an occasional stare. I was getting a kick out of watching guys play sports, and seeing them sweat; and staring at the bulge in their pants. I finally thought I had control over these emotions, and didn't have to worry about them controlling my life anymore. Then out of nowhere - my grandmother died. My grandmother was never the type of women to show any signs of weakness. You would never know if she was sad, sick or in pain. When my grandmother took ill, I was so confused because I've never seen her sick once in my entire life. I just knew she was immune to any and all illnesses. When she was sick, the vibe in the house was so different. She wasn't herself and for the first time, I was able to see right through her, and I knew once she went to the hospital; she wasn't coming back home.

And that's exactly what happened.

If you've seen the movie *Soul Food*, then you know how important this woman was to me. She was the air that I breathed. My angel on Earth. My earthly mother. I felt like my world had just ended….like seriously there was no reason to continue living without her. We all lived together, but I spent more time with my grandmother. My mother worked nights, so she and my grandmother would tag team on taking care for me. I was always with my grandmother in the kitchen when she would cook, or when she went out to meet male friends. The men fell to her feet and worshipped

28

the ground she walked on. She wasn't an average women, she was phenomenal. Men didn't disrespect her, and if they did, she would tell their asses off. I learned so much from her and she was taken away from me without warning. I was so lost. I didn't know what to do or how to carry on without her. She was *(my everything)*, and now I needed more love and attention. My grandmother was what I wanted my mother to be for me. She raised me when my mother went to rehab to get her life back on track. What I loved most about my grandmother is she was such a cheerleader for my mother. I know my mother didn't see it, but my grandmother told me every day how proud she was of my mother. I wish she would have said those words to my mother, because I do believe those words would have helped with her healing process.

She was the only lady who loved me for me.

I didn't have to hide who I was around her, because she already saw me. I believe my grandmother already knew the life I was going to live once I grew up. When I was with her, I stayed fresh! The best and latest fashions, hair always done, she was the biggest *Chicago Bulls* fan ever, so I was always wearing Bulls paraphernalia. She was the one person who told me always be the best you that you can be, and the amazing people that are meant to be in your life; will follow. No judgments came my way from her. She saw at an early age, that I was meant for the arts and she took advantage of that. She booked me for commercials, photo shoots and any time a speech was needed at church; she always signed me up. Between her and my mother, this wasn't your regular Easter speech, this was the audition of my life. I had to practice and practice every day, until I had the speech memorized. Then I would record myself to make sure I had the right amount of cuteness to go along with the seriousness of the speech. She introduced me the arts, so how am I supposed to continue on without her?

After my grandmother died, I think my mother lost the fire to go on with life without needing validation from a man. I lost the fire to go on period. My mother started using drugs again and began dating one of the worst men to ever come into our lives. I was always suspicious of him from the moment I met him. He was a grown man with a fat ass and enjoyed wearing tight pants. He had finger waves in the new millennium and got his hair done on a regular basis. I really couldn't stand this man, but my mother fell in love with him early in their relationship. My baby sister was very young, so she latched onto any man she came in contact with. He had everyone in the family under his weird spell.

Except me.

I knew he was an undercover sissy, I just couldn't prove it. He didn't really have any male friends, and the ones he did have, were suspect as well. I wasn't able to tell my mother any of this, because I knew she wouldn't believe me. So one night I decided I was going to get me some proof. One day I asked if I could ride with him into the city to go to his **"cousin's house"** *(this was a strange request coming from me, because he knew I didn't like him)*, but he agreed *(because he didn't want my mother to get suspicious)*. We drove all the way to the west side of *Chicago*. I loved the drive, because I can remember the summer breeze blowing in the car, and his old school music playing. One thing I did like about him was his love for *Toni Braxton*. After driving for a while, I fell asleep in the car. I woke to darkness and sweat pouring off my face. My skin was sticky on the leather car seats, an indication that I had been in this position for quite some time. The car was parked on a quiet block, which was unusual for that side of town. I was afraid to open the door and get out the car, because I wasn't sure if he put an alarm on. I was really hot, so I just opened the door and hoped it wouldn't make a sound. I recognized his voice coming out of one of the houses, so I started walking toward that house to see what was going on through the window.

What I saw was a surprise...

While looking through the window, I was upset when I saw him using drugs and drinking a lot of alcohol. This behavior didn't surprise me however, because I knew this was what he and my mother had in common. Inside, I was pretty angry, because I knew if he and my mother stayed together for a long time, nothing good would come from this relationship. I was about to go back to the car, when I saw a half-naked woman come into the bedroom. She sat on his lap, while he grabbed her ass and sucked on her breasts. She began to moan loudly, as he put his fingers in her panties. Then I saw him eyeball someone on the other side of the room that I couldn't see. I tried to move to the opposite side of the window to see who he was looking at, without him noticing me. As I moved to the other side, I saw the person he was staring at, and that person was a man. I was shocked when I saw him and forgot where I was, and let out a horrified scream. They jumped up and started putting on clothes and cleaning up the room. I ran back to the car and pretended like I was asleep. I was trying to adjust myself in the car before he came out, because I was so turned on by what I saw. While I was watching them, I wasn't really thinking about my mother's feelings or the pain she would endured if she ever found out.

I was thinking about how I could have been included in what was going on in that room.

Again, I am not sure why I felt this way but I had to do something about it before he came back to the car. I started by putting my hands in my pants and playing with myself. I closed my eyes and imagined that, I was the girl who got on top of him, and that his hands were in my pants.

Until…until… until…I came all over myself in the car. After that it was easy to go back to sleep and wait to get home.

Part of me wanted to tell my mother what I witnessed, but I didn't know how. She was happy and I loved seeing that smile on her face. But he just cheated on her and who knew how long this had been going on, or how many other women he had. My mother was at the point she was so deep in love, I was sure she wouldn't believe me if I told her anyway.

From that point on, I didn't have a problem with him because I felt like I understood him more. He was a man that had a lot of sexual juices flowing inside of him, that he needed to release. Now, I've never seen him have sex with a man, but I didn't doubt that he hadn't done it once or twice. He was a strong man, with a job and a family, but he still couldn't fight the urges his body craved. I could relate to him even more as years went on.

Oh yeah…my mother married him.

"Damn that feels so good.

Your touch makes me shake,

I don't know why but I like your touch.

My dick stands up watching you,

I really don't know what I'm doing

But the fact that you're moaning must mean I am doing something right?

Something is oozing out and it got on my lips.

It's not a lot though...

Is this the big finish?

Maybe not because you're still fucking hard.

I'm trying to remember to move my teeth...

Is that why you're saying, "Ouch?"

I don't want to hurt you

Let's stop and just kiss.

Damn are we even kissing right lol?

Let me use my tongue like I saw in the movies.

You're stroking me while I stroke you....

Damn that tickles in a good way...

...Wait I hear someone

Pretend you're asleep....

"Turn and face the wall" I don't want her to see us in the same bed....

"Let me get on the floor".....

A lady peeks in and says "Are y'all sleep?"

We don't say anything.

She closes the door and walks to her room.

By now our dicks aren't hard anymore.

We're scared.

"Shit if our grandmother caught us we would've been in so much trouble"

~

Chapter III: We Are Family - I Got All My Cousins with Me

Remember I said I was going to get back to this moment?
Remember my dad's definition of "quality time?" Ask me did I
mind....Hell No! As a kid, my grandmother's house was the place to be. I
would have a ball every time I was there. It was as if she lived in a central
location for all the kids in the area. There were about thirty kids on her
block, and we would stay outside until at least 9pm every night. Everyone
knew one another. It was like a daily block party. This wasn't only just
during the summertime, and weekends; but also after school. We would
walk to the park and play for hours. Most of the time, I really enjoyed
being at my grandmother's house. The women could cook, and we would
eat! (*As long as you didn't care about having high blood pressure or high
cholesterol.*)

I didn't know why it was called *"Sunday dinner"*, because my
grandmother cooked like it was Sunday every day of the week. There were
times I didn't like going to my grandmother's house, mostly because, even
though we were all family; the adults didn't like one another. Someone
was always fighting, getting drunk or going to jail. It became so bad, that
we (*the kids*) would take bets on who was going to jail or who was going to
get drunk that night. **One of my uncles actually went to jail for raping
his own daughter in my grandmother's house**. Amidst all this chaos, it's

understandable why our cousins felt the need to stick together. My grandmother had seven children of her own, but she was also the custodial parent of her niece's children. Two of them were the same age I was. One, was younger than me, and the other one was the baby. Grandma's *(biological)* grandchildren called them *"crack babies"*, referring to their mother and how they are always crying and had temper tantrums. That didn't mean anything to me because, I was really close to them. One of them, a girl was hilarious, she was like the sister I never had. We did everything together. Watched movies, sang songs, danced like crazy people, and even *"feminine"* things - like braid one another's hair. I wasn't afraid to be myself around her because being myself was so normal when we were together. We would play dress up games and even play *Jerry Springer*. Our birthdays were a day apart, so we would always celebrate together. Now my male cousin, *(her brother)* was my heart and we were close in more ways than one. He taught me a lot growing up. He taught me how to play basketball, and even helped me with my first sexual experience with a girl. Her name was Dominique, and she lived on the same block as my grandmother. I really wasn't attracted to her, but my cousin said I needed to know how the inside of a pussy felt. That intrigued me, so I agreed. I didn't know what the fuck I was doing. I just knew what noises she was supposed to make based on *HBO after Dark (Real Sex)*.

Now you know, *HBO after Dark* was amazing. I learned a lot about sex from watching that network. I never really saw a lot of black people having sexual experiences on the network, however I learned what sucking dick meant from watching it; and how women had orgasms. It was very interesting to see people live free with their bodies, and not care about the judgments of other people. I met her at this park we all used to go to. She said I was a cute chubby boy, and she wanted to kiss me. I didn't know the right thing to say or do. So I kissed her. She bit my lip and I was instantly annoyed by that, yet somehow, I became aroused thinking about my male cousin. He wasn't your ordinary eleven-year-old. He was a cool guy and all the girls wanted to be with him. I would sometimes try to peek at him while he was naked in the shower....I wouldn't dare tell him that I liked him in that way.

Darkness fell as I waited at the park with her. By this time, I think she figured out that I wasn't going to make the first move. We were sitting on the slide, and I was looking at the stars; as she was looking at me *(I didn't know why)*. After a couple hours I said, *"Fuck it, let's fuck."* I didn't know what the hell I was doing, but I was still aroused thinking about my cousin. This was perfect because she actually thought I was hard thinking about her - which made her excited and aroused as well. I wasn't surprised that she knew what she was doing, since her mother and older sister were well known whores around the neighborhood. What did have me confused, was the fact that she was moaning before we even did anything. I knew this chick was weird, but I didn't know how much until that moment. She claims she saw her sister having sex, and she was moaning for no reason; and she thought that was the most important part. Really, I was just ready to get it over with, because it was getting darker; and I knew I had to get back to my grandmother's house. I couldn't leave because I wanted to impress my cousin. Show him that I could have sex just like he could with a girl *(even if this was not who I wanted)*. I was still thinking about him, when she pulled down my shorts and sat on top of me. She slid down on top of me. As she started moaning, I started screaming. The sensation of her vagina against my skin disgusted me. I pushed her off of me, pulled up my shorts and ran back to my grandmother's house. As I ran home, I was so embarrassed and upset that I couldn't make myself have sex with her. I always thought it would be hard for me to find a girl, because of my weight, and here I actually found one; and I couldn't make myself do it.

This was the moment I realized I was truly gay, and I was freaking out.

What the hell am I going to tell my cousin?

I couldn't tell him that I didn't go through with it.

He would kick my ass.

Or call me a faggot.

I arrived at my grandmother's house, and noticed the house was dark and there were no cars parked outside *(It was a Wednesday night, which meant she and my other cousins went to church).* I decided I was going to lie, and tell my cousin that Dominique freaked out, and decided not to do it. Or that someone came to the park and made us run away. My heart was beating fast. I didn't want him to make fun of me or judge me. I knew he was home, because he never went to church. I walked in through the back door, and as I walked through the kitchen, *(which, smelled of my grandmother's fried chicken)* I grew anxious anticipating the conversation I would have with him. I made my way upstairs to the room he shared with his younger brother - the same room I slept in when I would visit. As I walked upstairs, I heard a girl moaning loudly. I thought it was my older cousin who always had some girl over to my grandmother's house to have sex. I began to walk up the stairs faster, because I was curious to see who the girl was. As I approached the top of the stairs, I heard my cousin's voice moaning and it stopped me dead in my tracks. Now I really wanted to know who the hell this chick was. The floor creaked beneath me as I walked closer to the door. I heard him jump and pause the *VCR*. He called my name and told me to come in. I slowly walked into the room, and asked him what he was doing. He began to talk as my eyes wandered...

Down. Down even further.

"Wow... Is that your penis?" I said with excitement.

He looked down, and with a nod answered yes. *"What's wrong with it?"* He asked.

"Absolutely nothing cuz" I replied.

His shorts fell slowly to the floor, and I was amazed at the sight of him.

I didn't think a twelve-year-old boy could have a penis that looked like that.

Its length, dripped wetness down his leg. I was instantly hard staring at him... He looked down and saw that I was excited too.

" Do you want to keep watching the movie with me?" he asked, I nodded yes, and sat on the bed next to him. I felt weird yet relieved sitting next to him on the bed. I had dreamt of this moment, but I never thought it would happen. He was shaking and was just as nervous as I was.

You would think that we would have been afraid of getting caught.

Yet, it wasn't that.

We were afraid of hurting one another.

Our outer thighs touched and my body grew more open and vulnerable. We both were rock hard by this time. My dick was so hard it hurt....I couldn't believe it.

His dick was so hard, it jumped repeatedly on its own. He stood up to turn the movie back on. He was watching a black porn film that featured voluptuous black women being fucked by dark skinned men with big dark dicks. As the movie began, I saw my cousin staring at the woman's pussy, while I stared at the guy's dicks. I'd never seen dicks that big in my life. There was this one guy with dreads in his hair, and very dark skin. He started eating the girl's pussy. Then she climbed on top of him backwards, and began sucking his dick; while he was simultaneously eating her pussy. I didn't know the name of that move at the time, but I sure as hell wanted to imitate it.

I started to tingle a bit and become really aroused.

That's when I realized he was stroking my penis.

It felt really wet and slimy, yet felt so good.

I couldn't believe what I was feeling in that moment.

I didn't want it to stop.

I wanted him to feel as good as I felt. We started watching the movie again. I saw her sucking the dread hair guy's dick. She spits on it and put it down her throat, until she began to gag on it. I thought it was gross, but he was moaning loudly as a result of it, which meant that this was something he liked. I wanted to try something, while he was stroking me...so I did. I turned, got down on my knees, and put his dick in my mouth. At first, I went slowly, and noticed that he was moaning. I was doing really well I thought to myself. Then this creamy looking stuff squirted in my mouth, *(it scared me and made me bite down on his dick)* which made him scream. I felt so bad because he was in so much pain from me accidentally biting him. *"Are you okay?"* I asked. His response was: *"of course not....you just bit my dick"*

"What was that - that squirted in my mouth?" I asked

"Pre cum..." He replied,

"Pre cum? What the fuck is that?" I thought to myself.

What followed was an in-depth discussion about pre-cum, regular cum and all things in between. He knew I had never had sex before, and he explained a lot to me that night. I started to talk to him about the girl in the park, and how it felt so wrong. He understood and started to laugh. We talked for the next couple of hours.

Rubbing up against each other.

Touching and licking each other.

I was finally relaxed and comfortable, and was ready to try again. This time we kept the television off, because we had to hear if a car was pulling into the driveway. At that time of day, anyone could show up to my grandmother's house.

Somehow, we didn't care.

We literally gazed into each other's eyes. I felt more ready than ever to go down on him. I told him to lay down as I started to go down on him slowly. This time I just listened to his body, and let my mouth move with it. My mouth started to become dry, so I let the saliva fall out my mouth onto his dick. I began going down as much as possible. I was so caught up in the moment, I forgot who he was. I heard him moaning over and over again. His knees buckled and his toes curled *(which turned me on)*. He licked his hand, and reached down to stroke the tip of my penis. It felt so good that I moaned while he was in my mouth.

It was getting so hot.

Then we heard a car pulling up. *(It was my grandmother, because we heard the other kids in the car)*. This didn't stop us, because it was too late, and we knew it would take her a while to come into the house. He started

moving his body deeper into my mouth. He gave one final shake and

moved my head. That's when the white cum started oozing from his dick.

His eyes were rolling and his body was shaking as he was cumming. I felt

a warm sensation go through my body. I remembered him stroking me as

well. I turned and looked down. I couldn't believe what I was feeling. I

wanted so badly to tell him to stop.

Because nothing should feel this good.

I grabbed his chest, because I had just cum on his stomach. We heard our

cousins running upstairs, so he quickly jumped onto the bed, and I stayed

on the floor with the blanket over my face *(that was stained with our cum)*.

My cousin entered the room and saw we were both asleep. She stayed at

the door for a while, because she noticed the television was off, but the

VCR was still on. I knew exactly what she was looking at and I prayed she

wouldn't walk over and turn television on. As she walked closer to the t.v.

I heard my grandmother call to her, *"Come downstairs your mamma is*

almost here." She closed the door and went downstairs. We both jumped

up, laughing and put on some clothes. That was an amazing experience that

we would remember forever. It went on for the next five years. Each time

was more intense than the last. *That moment changed both of our lives....*

forever.

You scream and shout at me

Full of anger and misery,

Because I am a man in love,

With another man as if my heart obeys my every command.

Every day fight against the tears, the anger, and the fear,

That today is the day that I'll be judged,

For how I feel and who I love.

Do you think I chose this life?

Do you think I want to fight?

Alone,

With no one to call on?

All my friends have left me behind,

Because I've decided

To truly be me.

Gay means happy,

But every day I am sad

Men fantasize about being with me,

But don't have the guts,

To make it a reality.

Men love the fact that I'm not what they have at home.

I'm their home away from home.

But I'm not where their heart is.

It would be easier if I were white.

White men book roles,

White men get jobs when they walk through the door.

And white men find love,

Because they have less baggage in their past.

But hey what do I know?

I'm just a lonely gay black man.

Chapter IV: Saved by the Bell

High school was a really hard time for me. I thought I would be ready to step into the big leagues, however, now in addition to knowing that I was gay, *my home life and starting a whole new chapter with some old friends and possible some new ones* was terrifying me half to death. What I was most afraid of was that I wouldn't fit in with some of the kids. It's not that I wanted to be popular, I just wanted to stay under the radar and avoid getting bullied. My mother was still using drugs heavily, so asking her for money to buy clothes and new Jordans was out of the question. Most often, I went to school with shoes so bad, I could feel the ground beneath my feet. At that time, I always thought it was because my mother didn't make enough money to take care of the entire household on her own. However, she supported her drug habit and her man's drinking with no problem at all. By the time I was a freshman, my mother had a whole basketball team of men coming in and out of our lives. I gotta say, my mother had awesome taste in men. I still believe she was in denial following my grandmother's death, and using drugs and having sex was the only way she could cope. One guy she met was a sexy ass redbone - with green eyes. I mean he had such an amazing body and he treated me like a son. He would walk around the house with nothing on like *Ving Rhames* in *Baby Boy*. I mean, he could have been with a twenty year old chick, but instead he chose to be with my mother. A woman working full time with her own house is a great catch to someone working part time in the liquor store. She ended up having a baby with this guy. I really didn't want to be a big brother. I didn't want to share what little time I spent with my mother, with this new baby. I also knew that her having this baby with him, meant he wasn't going anywhere for the rest of our lives. When my sister was born, I adored her and swore to protect her. I was even given the honor of naming her. After my sister was born, I never got the attention I wanted from my mother. She only seemed to have room for three things in her life: Sex, drugs and my baby sister. I wasn't angry because I knew she loved me. I had so much I wanted to tell her, and I never got the chance. Some nights I listened to her having sex. I waited for that moment to scream, so she would come running into my room to see if I was okay. I did this quite often. After a while, she blocked out the screams. She became deaf to them. My mother no longer showed interest in me.

I'd heard so many rumors about how they treated freshmen, like throwing pennies at them, steal their lunch money, or even worse beat their asses. I was terrified to walk through those *Trojan* doors, but I did it anyway. What softened the blow was that I had some loyal friends, who I knew from junior high. We all came over to high school together. They were loyal to a certain extent. See, all my friends had adapted to the social hierarchy *(the unwritten rules of high school).* They came dressed fly every day, had

boyfriends or girlfriends, and joined the right clubs and never ate the free

lunch. The only reason I believe I still had those friends, was because they

were trying to find some other way to fit in, besides the clothes they wore.

When I first walked through the doors of high school, I tried to find a way

to blend in. I was eager to see some of my friends, and to hide my

sexuality.

I noticed mostly all the upperclassmen were fine as hell. Everyone was

light skin with curls, baggy jeans with **K-Swiss** or all white **Air-Force**

Ones on. I don't think I was ready for this. I was so focused on trying to

blend in and not get my ass kicked. I was prepared to be incognito, but that

was impossible with all this eye candy floating around here. I met up with

a lot of my friends, and we caught up on the summer and compared our

class schedules. I felt so out of place during this time in my life, because I

had to hide everything that was going on in my life. I couldn't be a part of

the real conversations my friends would have. Especially about my new

found understanding of my sexuality, or about what had taken place with

my cousin - or the craziness going on at home. I just smiled and laughed

and said *"Oh nothing much, same old same old"*, yet inside I had so much

to say. I didn't know who I could trust. Yes these were my friends, but

people are quick to say they are your friend, and once you give them some information their loyalties tend to shift. As freshman year went on, I became less and less happy with myself. I was having sexual arousal moments from looking at guys and their bodies. It was also difficult not seeing my cousin anymore, and dealing with being overweight. I never considered my weight an issue, until other people made an issue out of it. I was constantly teased in school about my weight and my looks. At the time, I had long hair and I either wore it in braids or a ponytail. So instantly, I was called a *fat girl* or an *ugly boy*. My clothes came from a department store and not a mall, my mother dropped me off at school in a van and not the latest *Impala* or *Grand Prix*. Kids can be so cruel, and the only way I survived this difficult time, was to laugh at my own flaws while they made fun of me.

People change in high school. The same friends I started the semester with, slowly became part of my past. I thought I couldn't survive high school without friends, so I knew I needed to start fitting in; so I could make new ones. My goal was to tell a few people my secret.

That I was gay.

I never really had any male friends, because I wasn't athletic. Girls gravitated to me naturally, so I knew the girls were the friends that I needed on my side. One day, I was sitting in science class, and I was talking to a girl I'd known for a long time. I decided to tell her I was gay. I thought about this for a while. I just knew this was going to be an amazing opportunity for me to actually tell someone the truth. Let's just say this didn't go as well as I had planned. I sat down with my friend and we started talking about my sexuality, and why I felt this way, and how long I'd had these feelings. The conversation seemed to be going in the right direction. She was both understanding and curious at the same time, so I kept talking. Then she asked me about my crushes in school. I really didn't want to go into detail about the guys that I liked, because I'd never expressed these feelings to anyone...EVER!

Maybe this was the time to finally get those feelings out....so I thought.

I began to tell her what I thought their dick sizes were and what I thought they might be working with down below. I don't know what the fuck I was thinking. I went to junior high with her, and so she knew some of the guys' names. I mentioned this one guy who was an upperclassman. He was a senior and there was something about him that got me so hard every time I saw him. His name was Michael, and Michael looked like a dark chocolate candy bar, and an old school soap opera stud all rolled into one. I never spoke to him, never had any interactions with him. Why would I? He was a senior, but I did see him every day. He simply took my breath away, and of course I decided to say all of this to my friend. She was so intrigued.

She laughed and even agreed with me about how fine he was a few times. I don't think there was a single girl in that school who didn't find him attractive, unless she was a lesbian. So I felt reassured by this and I wasn't at all embarrassed.

Later that day I was walking through the halls and noticed a lot of people looking at me funny and laughing/whispering when I would walked by them. This was nothing new to me, so I assumed it was just them teasing me again. Someone I was really close to came up to me and said *"Wow Cordaro, I always thought you were probably gay, but I didn't know you liked every boy we went to school with."* I felt so numb. I was in complete shock. I didn't know how to respond to this revelation. So many thoughts were going through my mind, like, *"OMG! OMG! HOW THE FUCK DOES SHE KNOW? WHO ELSE KNOWS? I'M SO RUINED....NOW EVERYONE KNOWS! HELP JESUS! HELP!*

Then I said *"I don't know what you're talking about, but that's funny."* Then she went into detail about everything I told my friend earlier. She started talking about the dick sizes, me sucking them off, their bodies and how they made me feel, *(especially Michael)*. I was sweating and shaking as she spoke the exact words I'd used in the conversation with my friend....I didn't know how to respond.

So I ran to the nearest bathroom. I stayed in there for an hour. I missed class, and lunch, because I couldn't believe that my secret was out and spreading around school. This was not the way I wanted to be remembered in the first semester of school. I exhaled a few more times, and braved the high school halls once again, thinking that perhaps someone else's situation had captured their attention; and I was considered old news.

No such luck.

When I emerged from the bathroom, my secret had become part of so many stories. It had reached everyone in the school. I felt like I was in the scene from *Mean Girls* when everyone stared at the girls as they walked down the hall. They were calling me a: *'faggot'*, *'fat sissy'*, *'fat girl sissy'* and a *'fucking faggot'*. I walked into class feeling emotionally exhausted trying to remove tons of negative energy and fear that was coursing through my body. I went to gym class, walked into the locker room, and the guys began to move away from me like I had the plague. This behavior from the guys I didn't know really didn't surprised me. However, I was hurt and disappointed seeing guys I had gone to elementary school with acting the same way.

I played the part

I had male friends so no one would be suspicious.

I played sports during recess.

I talked and laughed about girls.

There were even a couple of girls I really liked, so I guess hearing this news was hard for them too…. but why treat me like this? I hadn't changed. I was still the same person they knew from before. They treated me like a foreigner, who didn't understand English. Honestly, it didn't matter whether I understood English or not, because their actions showed me exactly how they felt. In that very moment I wanted to die. I didn't see the point of living. I refused to go through life having to deny who I was because it made everyone else uncomfortable…. But I had no choice. Even though I wanted to end my own life, I refused to put my family through that pain and give the people who hated me so much satisfaction. That day just kept getting worse and worse for me. I was in math class when the guy I was crushing on *(Michael)* came into my class. I was about to shit a brick. I just knew he was coming to whoop my ass. I heard that word got around about all the people I told my friend I was crushing on, and he was at the top of the list. He walked in the classroom and walked right up to me - and I swear I almost peed on myself.

I became aroused. He was so fine. I just knew he was going to kick my ass.

He looked at me and said, *"Have you seen this guy named Cordaro?"* I looked confused as fuck, because clearly I was the guy he was looking for, and I was wondering why he didn't already know this information. I looked down and saw that my id badge was turned the opposite way, so he couldn't see my name.

I looked at him and said, *"He went home early."* He said *"Okay. Thank you pretty lady."*

I was going fucking crazy by now, but it all made sense. I was wearing my hair straight at the time, so this nigga thought I was a girl. As he left, all I could do was thank God for sparing my life. The school year had just started, and already I wanted to crawl under a rock. I was going home every night lying to my mother. Telling her I had a great day at school, when in reality, I just cried in the bathroom; and kept hiding from guys who wanted to beat me up. Every day during my fourth period class, I would ask if I could leave ten minutes early for the bathroom. I actually wanted to get to my locker, gather all my shit, and start walking home before any of the guys came out of class. My fourth period class was on the fourth floor, and my locker was all the way on the first floor- so I stormed down those stairs like *Jesse Owens* every day. I knew if I was in that hallway when everyone came out of class, I would get jumped. This became my daily routine. It was exhausting and overwhelming all at the same time. I was tired of running, but I didn't know what else to do. I stole money from my mother's purse every day, so I could eat burgers and nachos like the kids with money. I would also have to buy a random guy's food - so I wouldn't get beat up. I was uncomfortable around kids my own age. I would talk shit about them, but the upperclassmen had authority and a presence in school. I just knew that they would kick my ass.

No one would help me.

*Even the people I called my **"friends"** wouldn't help me.*

They didn't want to be associated with the fat gay boy. School became harder and harder for me to bear. The semester was almost over, but I couldn't keep leaving class so early. A lot of these guys were actually hurt that I came out and that for the past couple of years they were associated with me. One day as I was sitting in my English class, we received breaking news about two planes that crashed into a building in New York City. I wasn't sure if it was real or not, because it sounded kind of fake. Nothing about the story made any sense to me. I thought it was a plot of a new movie. . It looked so unreal.

Unfortunately, it was very real.

The planes hit the Twin Towers that day, and a lot of people died. In that moment I understood exactly what a terrorist attack was. A lot of kids were scared and for good reason. A lot of rumors started going around that Chicago would be next, so the principal decided to let us out early. All the buses returned to the campus and school was officially dismissed. Everyone started walking to their lockers in tears or in shock *(of course there were others who were just excited to leave school early)*. As I walked to my locker, I was pushed by someone and then I realized who it was.

Fuck.

This is my first time at my locker around all the other guys who wanted to fight me. I turned around and looked at this guy square in the eyes. I was surprised, because he was one of the few who I thought didn't have a problem with me coming out. He started calling me a *faggot*, a *loser*, and a *fat ass*. My mother was a *crackhead*, a *slut* and I was only gay because girls wouldn't fuck someone with such a small dick. People began to slowly stop walking past us....They were listening to what he was saying to me. I looked around. No one said anything to me. Some people looked hurt by what he was saying to me and some people laughed because they thought it was funny. Some people, however, did agree, yet they still thought it was mean. Then there were those who loved watching every minute of my humiliation in front of the entire school. I felt so belittled. I felt like the black slaves I had read about in our history books that were sold on the market. I was on display in front of all my peers, and no one stepped up to stop him. The principal called for the final bus and everyone walked away. Even the guy who was harassing me walked away.

As I was left alone in the hallway, I fell to my knees and began to cry. Up until that point I refused to let anyone see me cry, but I just couldn't take it any longer. ***Why was this happening to me?***

Just because I wasn't into women?

Because I was fat?

Because I was different?

I was the same Cordaro.

Nothing had changed.

I was being treated like an outsider. I was always the one who laughed when I saw others being bullied, but I'll tell you - It's not funny being on the other side. I picked myself up off the floor, and went to the principal's office because I knew I couldn't take it anymore. I had reached my breaking point.

I was either going to kill myself, or kill someone else.

Once I arrived at the principal's office, I told her everything that had been happening to me thus far. The principal made the worst suggestion possible, and I thought she was the dumbest person I'd ever met. She suggested that I bring my mother in, which meant I would have to tell my mother I was gay. I laughed in her face, and told her no! I told her what was going on at home, and how that would be a terrible idea. The principal was concerned that I didn't have a support system at home, and if I kept going along with the behavior of my classmates - having no one to talk to about it- I would self-destruct. Then she said I had to tell my mother and bring her in, or she would do it for me.

I left her office feeling like I'd just made matters worse. The principal wanted my mother to come in the next day, so I had no choice but to tell my mother when she picked me up from school. I was still in shock over what happened today in New York and I was sad for our country. However, I couldn't even focus on that, because I was walking to my mother's car - about to tell her the biggest and most important secret of my life.

I started playing out the many possible outcomes of the conversation in my head. The best solution was her slapping me, throwing me out the car and making me walk home. So you can only imagine what the worst outcome was according to my mind. I got into my mother's car and she began talking about the terrorist attack, and how sad it was and how she knew something like this was going to happen sooner or later... She then began to ramble on about all the dust and screams she saw on the news once the buildings collapsed, and how surreal it was. She then started talking about the dinner she made, and how I'd have to stay in the house and watch my sister - because she was going to work…... *"MAMMA I'M GAY!"* I screamed! *(Just to shut her up)*. Silence and heavy breathing were the only sounds I heard. Then I looked into my mother's eyes and saw the tears running down her cheeks. The look of disappointment pierced back at me from her eyes, and I never forgot that look.

Some time had passed and my mother still refused to talk to me about the conversation we had months earlier. I let it go, because I knew that when she was ready to talk, she would let me know. Nothing about her behavior or the way she treated me really changed. I think she either already knew this about me or out of sight, out of mind was her thinking. School was even starting to get better, and I guess it was because I was old news. I really didn't give a shit anymore. I think I actually started to have a normal life…...*Everywhere but in church.*

I loved my church home, it was full of many kids my age and had so many events that catered to our needs. The only problem was this one particular young minister who always felt the need to give sermons about homosexuality. I mean all he talked about was *"God made Adam and Eve, not Adam and Steve."* I never understood why every time he step foot to the podium, that was the highlight of his messages. We did have a lot of teenage gays and lesbians in our church, and we all clicked very well. I was never offended by his comments, because deep down, I knew he *'busted it open for some young boys'.* We all knew this but no one ever talked about it. The only problem I had with him, was that he wasn't living his truth. He was a hypocrite. He built this facade that everyone liked, yet he was so caught up in it. I'm not sure if he even knew that he was gay. He was also our youth leader, so I couldn't escape him. I had to deal with him every week. I guess he was cute, but he was so arrogant - I couldn't even appreciate his looks. One particular Wednesday I went to church after a really bad day at school and at home. My mother was being great about everything, but I wasn't happy with the guys she was with. I got so upset one day watching her smile with her boyfriend, because behind that smile; I saw the pain. So I already had a heavy heart going into the service. He started preaching about letting go of the sin that has you tied down and not giving up. It was an awesome message, so awesome in fact, I began to cry. As I was leaving service, the minister grabbed me and pulled me into a room with two other ministers, and three of my other gay friends I went to church with. The minister started to pray over my head speaking in tongues. The other ministers pulled out oil and started throwing it all over the place speaking in tongues as well. My friends and I were looking at each other confused as hell, because we didn't know what was going on. I knew this had to do with the fact that we were gay. He began saying things like; *"I bind the spirit of homosexuality in this room"* and *"Lord, remove the worst sin that a person can have out of their lives".* I mean he was so serious about this exorcism that he was sweating and crying. I got to the point where I couldn't take it anymore, and I was over this foolishness. The more he prayed over me, the closer he got to me. Then I put my right hand on his shoulder and slowly went down his shoulder blade. His eyes opened slightly and he looked at me, still praying. My right hand then went to his chest and I felt his body moving in closer to me. At this point, everyone's eyes were closed. As my right hand went down toward his belt buckle, he stopped praying and told someone else to take over. At this point his eyes were open and he was staring into mine. He knew where my mind was going, which is why I felt his dick on me while he had oil on my head. I smirked and said, *"and you thought you could fool me"* I pushed him away, grabbed my friends and we left. We were all so disgusted by his actions, and how the church allowed him to serve in a position of leadership, after treating us this way. Church was the last place I thought I would be judged for my sexuality, but apparently I was wrong. While many black pastors condemn gays and lesbians from the pulpit, the choir lofts behind them often are filled with gay singers and musicians. Some male pastors themselves have been entangled in scandals involving alleged affairs with men. Some say pastors' hostility cuts hard against the history of how countless black churches have flourished. The virtuosity of gay singers, musicians and composers has been the driving force in developing popular gospel choirs, but the black churches decide to ignore this fact and just constantly promote hate to the LGBT community.

I'm not sure why gays like getting fucked in the ass.

It definitely doesn't feel like red fucking roses,

Or cupid shooting you with a bow and arrow.

The shit hurts,

And if you get a fuck boy who's lost,

You're gonna go away bloody...

Let's not forget that part

Chapter V: The Boy is Mine

A couple of years had passed by this time, and I was starting to get my life back on track. Well, if *"on track"* is what you want to call it. I was now a junior in high school and was considered an upperclassman. All of the people who used to make fun of me, were no longer attending the school....well, some of their dumb asses were held back, and they were now in the same grade I was. People respected me now. I'd found a voice for myself in school, and I was proud of that. I was now the *"funny guy"*, and no longer the *"fat gay boy"*. My sense of fashion, still left much to be desired, but I was very trustworthy and I was earning a lot my respect as a person. I also developed a strong love for acting and the stage was always calling my name. So, I decided to join the drama club, and I had just done **Grease the Musical** with rave reviews. I also joined the choir, so now, people were looking beyond my sexuality to see my talent. My grades were still not the best... mainly due to the all of the drama going on at home. By this time in my life, my mother was committed to one man. He had been around for quite some time now. She was also in a committed relationship with drugs and alcohol, and it was still taking a toll on our relationship. I had a job working at a nursing home, and every check was either going towards school stuff, or to my mother to help pay bills. Her guy didn't have a regular nine to five. He had his own window washing business. I wasn't mad at him, because he was a black man trying to be a successful entrepreneur. He was funny as hell, and he would make me laugh every chance he got. Yet, I still didn't want to like him very much. Part of me knew that he was bad for my family, but I had no one I could talk to about it. He made my mother happy, so I couldn't stand the thought of telling her - she had gotten it wrong once again. The fact that they were both functioning drug addicts scared me the most. Functioning drug addicts are ticking time bombs, and can go off at any moment. They think they have so much control, but in reality; they have no control at all.

And these two definitely did not.

I went along with everything, trying to keep the peace, but I knew the shit would hit the fan one day. At this point of my highschool career, I finally thought I'd found a group of friends who were actually good *"friends"* to me. Three of them in particular made my day every time I saw them. One, was Ava the school's best and brightest actress, the other, was Nikki our resident "funny girl" *(Who had a large following),* and rounding out our little group, was Dana, the one who taught me everything there was to know about sex; and appreciating myself at the size I was. Actually, they all had a huge following, and being friends with them, made me look good. I was respected by others because I was close to them. I didn't have any close male friends at the time, however the guys that I did know respected me as well. I started to have a normal social life. I had to babysit my sister so often that I didn't get a chance to go out unless I was still at school for a rehearsal.

Still, I wanted more.

I wanted to be a top notch bitch at school, and the only way to make that happen was to make everyone believe I had an amazing sex life. Now, I couldn't say that I was having sex with guys at the school, because I didn't want to relive the drama of freshman year. So I made everyone believe that I was dating a college guy, with other niggas on the side. I guess being a whore was the cool thing back in the day. I would lie and tell them I met them on a party line, and that they came to my house, and we would have mad sex for hours. I even lied to Ava, Dana and Nikki when I told them I was fucking guys in the school, because at this point, I knew I could trust them. Dana had a lot of sex, or just a lot of guys wanting to have sex with her, so she could most definitely relate to my conversations about it. I had to make sure all the details I provided her, were accurate; because she would know if I was lying. I'm sure she caught me in a few lies, but didn't say anything. I envied this girl. Not only did everyone like her, but her personality was everything!!!!!! I wanted to be her. She didn't let her size determine how her day was going to go and I believe this was why the boys liked her. We started hanging out and I really was determined to pick up some of her tricks, not just the ones about sex, but also fashion and behavior tips. She was always clean and well-groomed yet overweight. You could tell just by her presence, that she loved herself and the skin that God put her in and that contagious spirit started to fall off on me. She became confrontable with me and started telling me about her sexual encounters. I was so tuned into our conversation, but not just for the talk and laughter…

oh, no this bitch was taking notes

She talked about how she always watched videos, or clippings of women sucking dick wrong and how she knew that she could become a pro at it. I took all those notes and was practicing at home on banana's, pop-sickles, suckers…I mean hell, whatever I could get in my mouth. She told me the trick to sucking dick good was to make sure it was nice and wet and that I pushed my teeth back as far as possible. Apparently, guys didn't like their dick being sucked and your teeth grazing on it. She also informed me that once the dick nuts I must keep sucking, which is apparently a very sensitive moment for a guy.

I was so excited to receive all this information, but what was the point if I never got a chance to use it?

Dana had the greatest taste in men, I mean the greatest taste. She liked guys that were buff, pretty looking with a nice smile, which was the same for me. I don't know how she got the guys, but she always had a new number every single day. Other girls, who were pretty and big, still didn't get any action like Dana. I must admit there was a point I got jealous. I hated that every time we were out together or she wanted someone to ride with her to meet a guy I never had anyone to talk to. It was always about her every time we went out. I was so jealous that I was determined to take her next guy from her. At this point in my life friendship was important, but having a boyfriend who was very good looking was more important to me. I still couldn't be aggressive because I have been lying to her for so long saying that I was or have been in relationships.

How can you tell the truth to someone that has it all and doesn't even know it?

I liked to email some of her guy friends (see back then, yahoo instant messenger was very big and it was easy to get each other's email

70

addresses). I would steal their emails when she was logged into her phone or computer. I wanted these guys to talk to me the way they talked to her. I wanted them to want me the way I wanted them. She always showed me dick pictures and I would get so turned on by them that I had to experience it myself. The only way to achieve this was to pretend to be someone else so I can get their attention. It wasn't about trying to have sex with them, I just wanted to hear someone say I sounded sexy, even though I knew they were only talking to the name I gave them. That wasn't the point, the point was it made me feel good to hear it in my ears. I got goosebumps and excitement thinking that they really liked me, even though I manipulated the entire situation.

I knew this girl and I had a lot in common, we would finish each other's sentences, eat the same food, laugh about the same things and sing the same way. At some point, I started to see why we were so gravitated to each other. Especially when I knew she wouldn't have a boyfriend for a long period of time. She always had these men all over her, but none of them stuck around, but she always walked around with a smile on her face. I'm not sure if that smile was genuine, but she kept it. I believe she was looking for love in all the wrong places just like I were. Looking for a man to show her the love that her father, grandfather or other male family members couldn't give her. At some point, I thought she did find that kind of love. He was exactly the man I thought she would be with, hell he was the man I wanted to be with. Yet again, he still was another disappointment in the male species. Dana found out she was pregnant and she was over the moon excited and so was I. At this point in her life I do believe this baby was exactly what she needed to obtain the love she was looking for, unfortunately, she did not have the support from her baby daddy. She refused to get an abortion and was sticking with her guns that he loved her. That he would never kill his very own child. However, if he wanted her to get the abortion, he would have to pay for it. A little time had passed, she began to become hopeful about her future. She knew that this was not the way she wanted her fairytale love to begin, but the path she has taken thus far lead her to this road, so she walked it hitting every major roadblock that came her way. I'm sure that she was not expecting the next barrier that came her way. I can't tell her story because I believe it would be wrong to tell something so near and dear to her that a lot of people do not know, but my heart was hurting for her. I was angry, sad and numb that man could leave a woman and allow her to go through these moments alone. This asshole had the nerve to let her be depressed alone. Even though she was not gay, she was still dating, or trying to date men that had no desire to allow her being number one in their life. Again, we had a lot in common.

She had to go through it all alone and I wasn't even able to be there to support her, because I was still trying to find his email address for myself....

Now both Ava and Nikki were virgins, so I'm sure they didn't know if what I was telling them where facts or fictions. Ava was a very special part of my life, because I looked up to her. She was popular for just being herself. *She didn't try to fit in with a crowd, the crowd tried to fit in with her.* Her talent spoke for itself.

And all the guys wanted her.

I wanted so badly to be her.

We were close and we went everywhere together. Ava was very pretty, such a natural beauty, and sometimes I wondered if I was sexually attracted to her; or just envious of her. I'm not sure what it was, but I did know I wanted her boyfriend all to myself. He was on the football team, even though he looked like he should have been a mathlete. He was tall, skinny, wore nerd glasses, and he had a high-pitched voice; but he was very handsome. What I liked most about him was, he was cool with me being me. We just clicked. We had our own conversations, about any and every thing. I felt like I was in a relationship with him. My feelings were out of place, because I was good friends with Ava. The only thing I could ever think about - when we were together- was making the lies I was telling everyone about my sex life a reality with him. At the time, I wasn't sure if he was gay or just curious, but I wanted to be around him as much as possible to find out. I would jump at the opportunity when she would ask me to ride with her to his house. They had such a cute relationship. Ava would go over his house and sit in the backseat with him and talk all night or they would make out. At first, it felt weird being in the front seat, while this was going on, but after a while I tuned them out and enjoyed the *R&B* music on the radio. He speculated that I had a crush on him. I believed she knew as well. He didn't treat me any differently once he knew I was gay, but he would tease me; since I couldn't have him. He would make these comments while he was in the backseat making out with her. I got so aroused listening to them moan. They weren't having sex, however, their moaning transpired from two individuals who loved one another. When she dropped me off at home, I would lay in bed thinking about them - moaning, touching myself and making myself cum. I wanted that kind of love and attention so badly. One night while playing "co-pilot" on one of their many outings, we stopped at a park after it was closed. I didn't think much of it, since we randomly go to these kinds of places to chill and talk like anyway. This night was a little different, because they left me in the car to walk into the park. It surprised me because they didn't normally do anything if I wasn't around.

So, was this the night they would finally have sex?

I wouldn't have been surprised...the sexual tension between them was so electric, even I felt it. I saw them walk over to the slide, and I was instantly turned on by the possibility of what could happen once they sat down. It was well after 11pm, and the park was completely empty. You could hear the wind brushing up against the metal frames of the swings nearby. I lowered my window some more, and turned the radio down so I could hear well. Suddenly, I heard some muffled moaning far off into the distance. I couldn't pinpoint whether it was him or Ava. At that point I didn't care who it was. I just wished I could watch. She was a virgin and he was very inexperienced, so I knew their first time would be horrible.

I wanted to be part of it in some way.

I started touching myself and I just couldn't stop.

Damn, why couldn't it have been me with him while she sat in the car?

I bet his dick is long and beautiful.

She said he was an amazing kisser.

I bet he ate her pussy really good.

All these thoughts were running through my head, as I sat there stroking myself. I felt like I was getting closer to cumming, when I heard them walking towards me. I hurried to adjust myself, and turned the music up just a little. I was in the front passenger seat, so when she walked up she went to the driver's seat, which meant he had to pass my window; in order to get in the car....we made eye contact.

I wanted to tell them. So we all could get off.

Together.

Nikki was my other close friend who has stood by me since junior high school. She didn't dress like the popular kids or wear the latest fashion. Her personality was so big and bright...no one cared! We hung out together all the time, especially during the summer months. Most of the time I went to her house, and we would sit outside and watch guys drive past the house. We would laugh at them for being so damn ugly, or we would whisper about them being so damn fine. Like me, she had low self esteem, but she never showed it.

But I knew it was there.

I saw myself in her.

She was a big girl, with big breasts, yet she was very pretty to me. I mean this girl had huge breasts for a girl her age, and they didn't really compliment her figure. Her personality was to die for, and that was why I gravitated to her so much. Her appearance didn't matter to me, because I wasn't attracted to her, but I knew it was hard for her to accept herself. *She did and I loved her for it.* Sometimes, we would hop on the party line, and pretended to be these cute girls who wanted some company. I was always *Tiffani*, a light-skin, thick girl with long pretty hair. Her fake girl looked similar, only she was brown skin with curly hair. Guys would hit us up and try to come over to our house. We would give them fake addresses just to see how they looked if they showed up. We played this game almost every day. It was fun to be someone who somebody else wanted. This was before camera phones, and smartphones, otherwise our schemes wouldn't have worked. Some time passed, and I was busy with church and I didn't go to her house as often as I wanted to. I heard through the grapevine that she eventually met a guy. A real one - someone that actually liked her the way she was.

I couldn't wait any longer to find out the truth, so I walked to her house to see him for myself. I get there and he hadn't arrived yet, which was a good thing, because I wanted to get the dish on him before he got there. She was so happy and wore the biggest smile on her face. She told me he was in his early twenties, which concerned me. This girl was barely sixteen years old. She told me they met at *Big Boy's* restaurant, and that he approached her out of the blue. Judging by everything she told me, he seemed like a really cool guy. Suddenly, as we were still talking, a guy pulled up with his brother in a *Gray Bonneville*.

"Here he is." She said with excitement. He got out of the passenger side and started walking toward us. He was tall and skinny and quite funny looking. I could tell he had no swag whatsoever, yet something about him must have been very appealing to her. That night, I saw a different side of my friend. I saw a shy girl who was quickly falling in love with a guy she barely knew.

I saw myself in her yet again.

He seemed like a thug and I was worried about how our first encounter would transpire, due to the fact that I was gay. He walked up to me and I could smell the alcohol seeping from his pores. She stood up to hug him, and he grabbed her ass and buried his head in her chest, like he couldn't wait to hit that. She would've told me if they were fucking, so I assumed they weren't. Come to think about it, she did have a certain glow that a virgin would not possess. She introduced me to him and he stared into my eyes the same way he looked at her…..predatory, like an animal, ready to attack. I was so embarrassed by they way he looked at me, I had to quickly turn my head away from him. *"So you're the guy I heard so much about. I was starting to think you was her other nigga, the way she kept talking about you. But by the way you look, I can tell it's true, you are gay."* He

said. I was slightly confused. I wasn't sure if it was meant as a compliment

or an insult. However, under the current circumstances, all I could was

laugh it off. We all sat down on her porch, he was sitting between my

friend and myself. He told his brother that it was okay for him to leave, and

that he would walk back home later. Once again here I was playing the

wingman to a friend and her man...but I hung in there and just enjoyed the

awesome summer breeze. He had a couple of beers with him and had asked

us if we wanted one. We both declined. Then he popped open a can and

kept drinking. We were listening to some music and just chillin on the

porch. They started kissing and making out....I just sat there. As he leaned

in to kiss her neck, she closed her eyes, and began to moan softly. His right

hand started going up my leg. He was clearly drunk and confused, because

that was not her leg....it was mine. I moved quickly to my right, before she

opened her eyes. I wasn't sure what was happening.

I didn't like it.

A couple of hours passed, and I realized I had forgotten to ask my mother

to pick me up. I went into the house and tried to call my mother twice, but

there was no answer. So I decided I was just going to walk home. I wasn't

really worried about anyone bothering me, however, I was worried about a

skunk spraying me or running into deer. *(Sidenote: I'm afraid of Deer)* I went back outside and they had taken things a little bit further than I thought they would. Her right breast was out and he was sucking on it. *"I hate to interrupt...but I am going to start heading home, I'm going to walk".* My friend was a little concerned about me walking, so I assured her that I would be fine. Then her boyfriend insisted that he should be going to and offered to walk me halfway. She actually thought it was a good idea.

So did I.....

She lived near the woods, so there was no telling what kind of animal would have popped out of the trees. She gave him one final long kiss and then we left. The weather was quite perfect at 1am, surprising for a summer morning in Chicago. The walk started out pretty quiet. Then he started asking me questions about my family and how long I had been gay. I indulged him in the conversation, since he was nice enough to walk me halfway home. We started to walk into the forest preserve, because that was a quicker route to get home. It was getting darker as we walked through, so my scary ass started walking faster and faster. He told me to slow down because the night was too young to end so soon. I wasn't sure what the hell he meant, but it made me slow down. He said, *"I'm not ready to call it a night, how about you?"* *"I'm not either..."* I replied. He looked into my eyes and asked me what I wanted to do....my next words changed my life forever... *"It's whatever"* I guess these words were all he needed;

because in the middle of the grassy field, at two a.m. - my best friend's boyfriend kissed me *(He was just kissing her)*. He looked at me expecting a reaction. A normal person would've slapped him, or pushed him off - or told him the hell off for doing that. Not to mention how he was hurting Nikki. That would've been a normal response…..an internal response of sickness and disgust would have been the proper reaction, but that wasn't my response either. I actually enjoyed it. His kiss was warm and tender and felt so genuine. That kiss was everything I could have imagined and more. Even though it was a hot summer day, his kiss warmed my body like it was a cold winter evening. *Is this what I have been waiting for all these years? Was I finally getting a chance to experience something true?* Something that wasn't a lie I told my friends. I stared at him for a second and then I leaned in and began kissing him. Other than my cousin, I'd never kissed anyone before. Compared to this, that moment was nothing special. In the back of my mind I thought, I would feel bad for my friend, but in that moment…I didn't give a shit about her feelings. *I needed this to happen.* A person who thinks very little of themselves, allows someone to use them until they're useless. I'd never had anyone call me sexy or pay this much attention to me. It felt intoxicating and I needed to know what I could do to keep feeling this forever. At the time, the price I'd have to pay seemed reasonable….it wasn't worth it. I had sex with him in the woods that night.

It was my first time having *anal sex*. I was nervous when he kissed my

neck. My whole body tingled. With each passing moment, I felt his dick

growing harder and harder in his jeans. He pulled down my pants as he

kissed me. Then he licked his fingers and stuck one in my ass. I jumped

just a little, because I wasn't sure what he was doing and it felt

uncomfortable. *"Damn that ass is tight."* He whispered, I wasn't sure what

he meant. Is he saying it's tight as in it looked good? I was slightly

confused! He asked if I was a virgin, and I couldn't lie to him, so I said

"Yes." That instantly excited him and turned me completely around. He

pulled his pants down and rubbed his rock hard dick against my ass. I felt

the moistness of his pre ejacution. Baby, he was ready. I started to get

nervous when he tried to bend me over. So many thoughts ran through my

mind like: *was my ass clean?* I tried to remember the last time I went to the

bathroom. I didn't want my first experience to be my worst experience.

Yes, I was already thinking about the future. He bent me slightly over,

stroking my back, trying to relax me. He slobbered on his dick to make it

wet, so he could place it inside me. I kept tensing up. He kept telling me to

relax, but how could I? I was in the middle of the forest preserve at 2am

with deer and God knows what other animals running past me, any of

whom could get close enough to bite the hell out of me! My body tensed

up even more as he put his penis inside me….I was suddenly paralyzed.

Not because I was in heaven, but because it felt like I'd just crossed the threshold into purgatory. **THAT SHIT HURT!** I didn't yell or scream out loud, but my body did on the inside. He felt me tensing up, so he slowed down. I started breathing heavily, because him slowing down made me sigh with relief. He started going slower and deeper. At this point, I'd actually started to enjoy it. *"I'm in now,"* He whispered, and I realized that all of his dick was inside of me. I can't lie. The pain was real. *It also made me want more.* His strokes were getting longer, faster, and deeper. By now, I was trembling and I felt as if I had been mentally transported to another place. We were sweating and I felt his sweat dripping down my back, as mine fell to the ground. He didn't moan, but he was breathing heavily. At the moment when I was really enjoying myself he quickly pulled out of me, and I gasped really loudly. He was nutting all on my back and moaning so much as it dripped all the way down my leg. He had on two t-shirts, and took one off to wipe it up. I told him to leave the sweat because I was still in awe of the experience. *I needed to hold onto it. I needed a taste of it to know that it was real.* I straightened up and my back was sore. My ass was on fire! The image of me as I tried to walk made him laugh. We kept walking towards my house. During the rest of the walk home we were quiet. I guess he didn't know what to say. That was the moment when I realized that he had walked me further then he said he would. Honestly, after what just happened, I wasn't sure how to carry on a coherent conversation either. We stopped and stared at one another for a moment that felt like eternity. We were going in opposite directions. *"So what's next?"* I asked him. He looked at me and smiled, *"Nothing. You go about your business and I'll go about mine."* His tone and body language had changed dramatically as he spoke... *"I mean, let's be real... nothing is going to change. I'm still going to fuck your friend, and you're going to act like nothing happened between us or else."* Or else? *"Or else what"* I asked. Then he pulled out a gun from his pants pocket. He said, *"See, I knew you would understand."* I was shocked. How could the same person I just had this amazing encounter with, be the same person who was now threatening my life? He did a complete 180 on me that I didn't see coming at all. The most important moment in my life, had just been ruined and I couldn't tell anyone about it. *Who could I tell?* I'd just completely disrespected a girl whom I considered my best friend. He was disrespectful to both of us, and I couldn't tell her about any of it.

Yes, this was my first time so, it was something I would remember forever. I was also going to remember that my first lover, was also Nikki's boyfriend. So, he was not only an invader of my life and my heart - *I was now an invader of her life and her heart as well. Who wants to remember their first sexual experience was with the same person who cheated on you with your best male friend?* As I walked into the house, I was experiencing so many different emotions. I was still high from the sexual experience I'd just had, yet I was also afraid for my damn life. This man had just fucked the shit out of me, and then threatened my life - all in the same hour. The morning after was a bitch. I felt like I had the urge to shit so badly that I ran into the bathroom...nothing happened. I was very confused about why my farts felt like I was going to shit a brick. My ass was so sore, that I didn't know whether I should go to the doctor's office or just sit on the toilet and pray for healing power. I was online trying to see if he had torn something on the inside. *My ass was on fire!* My mother kept knocking on the door to see if I was okay. I just told her I had a few *White Castle burgers* the night before so she wouldn't worry *(We all know about those shit burgers right don't we?)*. My best friend kept calling me to talk about her man, and to ask if he'd said anything about her on the walk home. I ignored her calls, or told her that my mother needed to use the phone. I just couldn't lie to her. That is until I came up with a good lie and practiced it repeatedly in my head.

Why couldn't I just tell her the truth? Why couldn't I just say, *"I fell in love with your man. He was my first, and it was amazing."* Or *"Girl you can't trust niggas, because they lie and cheat on you like he just did."* Do you think she would have been happy, just because I just saved her from making a huge mistake and falling in love with this player? Clearly he wasn't feeling her, because he sung my way as soon as he had the chance. All these thoughts were running through my mind. I was sitting there trying to justify my part in the situation. I just couldn't. This was my friend who I've known since I was five years old. No matter how many times I tried to twist it around. *I was the guy who had sex with her boyfriend.*

Blame him...

Blame the alcohol....

I even blamed my own insecure behavior.

It was still wrong.

And I had to come clean.

Weeks passed and all I could think about was telling my best friend. I knew I would need some back up, because she was so in love with him. I would need some proof to support my claim as well. I decided to call the guy on three-way with a mutual friend who I knew would back me up. Even she was in denial when I told her what happened. She quickly changed her tune when she heard the conversation between him and me over the phone. He told me how proud he was that I kept my mouth shut, and how it had been a test to see how well I could keep my word. I mean it's not hard to keep your word, when you've been threatened with a gun, sir! He said the gun wasn't loaded and that he would never shoot me. He just wanted to make sure I took the situation seriously and that I would never tell his girl about it. He said that by telling her, I would lose both her as a friend and him as a lover. I had to think long and hard about this and I knew I didn't want to lose her. I couldn't risk losing the best sex I'd ever had in my life either. *Could I risk losing the only man who ever looked at me the way he did?* I said that he was right, but in the back of my mind I knew that I was going to tell my best friend. We ended the phone call and my other friend was in shock. She wasn't upset by my actions, however, she was simply shocked at the way he tried to justify the situation. We agreed that once I was ready to tell my friend, she would back up everything I said. Later that day, I went over my best friend's house, and he was already there laying down new tile in her kitchen. He worked doing odd jobs with his father and fixing up homes was one of those odd jobs. When he saw me, he smirked, and I wasn't sure what I was going to do. Clearly, I couldn't tell her the truth with him right there. Even though he told me the gun was just a scare tactic, I wasn't going to take the chance especially - while he was hanging around. I walked into her home and sat in the living room, while he was still in the kitchen working. She came in and sat down beside me and started whispering to me about the night before. She'd finally given him her virginity. She was so excited. She gave me all the dirty details. How his dick looked. The noises he made. The way he shakes when he is about to cum. I guess I couldn't keep a poker face very well, because she wanted to know why I wasn't surprised. Quickly, I came up with this lie... *"I'm just experiencing a stomach ache, and I'm really focused on the conversation....sorry."* It was better than telling her that this shit is old news to me. I already knew how he moaned and how he shook when he is about to cum. I could've said, *"Well girl that makes two of us!"* But of course I kept my mouth shut and just pretended to be happy for her. Suddenly, he emerged from the kitchen to be nosey and check on us. She went into the bathroom to take a shower and told both of us she would be right back. He wanted to join her in the shower, but she knew her mom would be home soon and she didn't want them to get caught. As she went into the shower and he heard the water turn on, he came and sat closer to me. He looked at me like he wanted to attack me, which kind of scared me. He moved closer and closer to me saying, how much he missed my tight ass, and how I better not give it to anyone but him. He started squeezing my thighs tightly, and even though I kept moving away from him, I was still getting turned on by his touch. He put his hand on my penis and told me to be still...he knew I didn't want to miss this feeling. I was so nervous that she was going to catch us, or her mom

89

was going to drive up. *But the anticipation made me want him even more.* He pulled his dick out and stood up by my face. It was rock hard and he told me to suck it. This was something I was really good at, so I was willing and eager to do it. I made it nice and wet and put my mouth on it very slowly. He told me to play with myself as I sucked him off....so I did. He liked it real slow, he wanted me to stare at him while I sucked it slow, so he could look at me and moan. I wasn't listening for the sounds of the shower to turn off or for her mom arriving home. At this point, I didn't give a fuck anymore. I was so focused on pleasing him and he definitely didn't care if we got caught either. What we should have cared about was whether the house was empty beside the three of us....because it wasn't. Actually her brother was asleep in the basement and we heard him making his way up the stairs. He quickly moved away from me, and ran out the front door. Her brother made it halfway up the stairs and then stopped and went right back down. My heart was beating so damn fast, I almost pissed myself. Not long after that, my friend got out the shower and walked into the front room. She received a call from her mother saying she was going to be late. She told me that she was going to be busy in the bedroom, because he was about to come in there. I said, *"Okay. How about I just go home?"* So as I was leaving, he came back into the house and went into her bedroom. Glad I was able to get the party started for them.

What was I going to do?

I couldn't keep this secret anymore.

It was getting too dangerous.

There must be someone I could tell who could give me some insight on how to handle this situation. *But who?* I went to school that fall still keeping my secret. I didn't know who I could turn to for help. The time came for me to tell my friend. Over the summer, her boyfriend and I had sex at least five more times, and it was better each time. I knew that she had sex with him too, because she would tell me about it afterwards. Sometimes we'd both have sex with him on the same day. He would fuck me in the morning and then go to her in the evening. He even told me that he had to think about me first before he had sex with her. This information became too much of a burden to bare, and I didn't know what to do. Our mutual friend who knew about this was on my side, and ready to back up my allegations. The problem was, we'd waited so long that now Nikki was invested in this man. How could Dana, our friend say *"Yeah I've known since the summer time."* She would definitely stop talking to her, so I decided to do it on my own, so not to involve anyone else. One day while at school, I was in class not feeling well, and I had a really bad ache in the pit of my stomach. I started talking to this girl who asked me what was wrong. Now this girl, wasn't just a random person. I'd known her for a while and she was someone I thought I could trust. I couldn't keep this secret any longer, so I told her everything that happened up to that point. I told her all about the weird love triangle I was in with my best friend. When I saw her jaw hit the floor, I knew I just made a huge mistake. To be honest, I could not stop talking. Telling her my secret felt like therapy to me. Holding all this back was eating me alive. It felt like I was a freshman all over again. As I expected, she was speechless after I told her everything. Then she laughed and said that no one would believe me anyway *(even if it were true)*. So, she said the best thing I could do was keep it to myself. So I did as she suggested. Honestly, by this time, I didn't see the point in telling her anymore. There were other rumors that summer about him and other girls, and she didn't mind those at all. *So why the fuck was I going to risk losing my friend and possibly my life?* I didn't expect the same bitch who told me to not say anything, to go and tell the entire school. **Never again.** I wasn't about to relive the same shit I went through freshman year. As soon I got to school the next day I was confronted by my friend. I'd been avoiding this moment for an entire semester. I thought to myself, here we go again. *"So you're just going to lie on my man like that?"* She asked me. The words *"Excuse me bitch?"* burst out of my mouth as she began to deliver her Oscar worthy performance of her life,

"How dare you lie on my boyfriend! He is not gay! He loves pussy. He could never be gay. He wouldn't mess with your ugly ass anyway!" (And my favorites quote of all) "Our sex is too good for him to be gay!" Not only would let me get a word out, but she also had a squad of friends behind her instigating the whole thing. She even had the nerve to say, that he told her I was crushing on him, and he told me to stop harassing him; or he would tell her all about it. I begged and pleaded with her not to do this in front of everyone in the school. I begged her to let me explain, but Nikki refused. I saw a puzzled look on her face, the face of a woman who knew everything she said was a lie.

Nikki knew. A woman always know

Nikki had the look of a woman who stared at herself in the mirror, as she made those comments about being and feeling ugly, and projecting them onto me. I saw a soul that was hurt, a soul who wanted to put on a show; without embarrassing herself....when in reality - she fell below the boundaries that we thought life had given us. *What could I say to her?* Apologizing would be the same thing as admitting it did happen, and the embarrassment she would've received; would have been too much for her to bare. So, I just let her yell and scream in my face. I felt like this was going to be our last encounter together anyway, so I wanted her to make it count. I was ready to be her punching bag, so she could get everything out that she needed to say. Our relationship was different after that, and so were my relationships with everyone else at school. Every day her girlfriends would make a big deal about me and this guy - not that it was true, but it was a desperate attempt for more attention. Sometimes I wasn't sure if it was a trap, or if she was setting me up to get my ass kicked by her brothers. This was more difficult than I thought, because she was protecting him from me. She actually convinced herself that it was impossible for him to be with another man. The only relationship that did not change was mine and his. I take that back, it did change a little bit. Our sex life became even more intense and interesting. I thought he was going to kill me for saying something to her, and kill me he did. We started rimming each other, kissing each other and enjoying each other's company. He convinced my best friend to forgive me and move on. Only because he wanted to have a better excuse to see me. People were calling me so many names. I became the face of what people hated about gay black men *"Why do people think that we make every straight man gay?"* In their eyes, I was a problem that needed to be fixed. I started having flashbacks of freshman year-when I was bullied for being gay. I didn't want that to happen, but every time I told him the cruel things people were saying about me, he would suck on my nipples and apologize for the fact that I had to go through so much. Sometimes while we were lying down, my best friend would call him and he wouldn't answer. I had fallen in love with this man, and I was okay with being the sacrificial lamb; if it meant that we could spend more time together.

Fuck her feelings.

My senior year in high school was a very difficult time for me. Unlike the rest of my senior class, I had no idea what I was doing with my future. I was so focused on being relatable to my peers, being liked, and surviving being bullied; I forgot that there was life after high school. My grades were shit. I didn't apply to any colleges or trade schools. I wasn't sure what I would do next. Everyone else I knew had major plans for their future, and there I was still trying to pick up the pieces of everything that has gone on over the past few years. I still didn't have a boyfriend or anyone to call my own. I was still fucking my best friend's boyfriend. I began to yearn for the relationship with him that I couldn't have. I wasn't enjoying just having sex, and then going out for dinner alone anymore. *Why did I feel so lonely, when I was in a relationship?* I'll tell you why, it was because, this wasn't the relationship I had prayed for. I wanted to be able to hold hands with someone, go to the movies and laugh; and eat out of the same popcorn bucket. None of that was going to happen as long as I was with this guy. I believe my friend and I were going through the same thing, because they weren't doing anything in public together either. I believe it was killing her just as much as it was killing me. Things at home were really heating up for us. My mother was really heavy on drugs and she just couldn't see herself working at her job any longer. She decided to take an early retirement instead of getting fired. She walked away with a lot of money and I wasn't sure if that was the best solution to the problem. My mother's boyfriend had a hold on her. The hold was stronger than I ever thought it could be. She was so blinded by love that she couldn't see how bad he was for our family. He never physically abused my mother....at least not in front of me, but psychologically, he was destroying her. At first, he was doing more drugs than she was, but the tables quickly turned and she became worse than he could ever be. They decided to take some of the money that she received from her pension and flip it - meaning they wanted to double the money by selling drugs, and not just any drugs. They decided to sell *crack cocaine*. I knew a long time ago my mother was using drugs heavily, however, I thought she stopped and was only smoking weed. I was amazed at how stupid my mother thought I was. Not too long after my senior year started, their operation began, and they started selling drugs. They teamed up with some guys who lived down the street from us, and planned to sell small amounts of crack to people in the neighborhood. They couldn't decide on a distribution location, so our home became the headquarters of their operation. At first it didn't seem that bad. They had some great money coming in from the sales, nothing major, but enough to keep all of our bills paid and food in the house. I started to receive more of the things I wanted like: new shoes, fresh clothes, *(which made me really happy)* and the latest electronic devices. Finally, I was able to enjoy my last few months in school looking like someone special. I also didn't have to worry about babysitting my little sister anymore, because with my mother at home, I was able to keep up with the school activities I enjoyed like: drama club and the yearbook committee. My mother even seemed happy with what she was doing, her man was doing most of the leg work, but she was definitely the mastermind behind the whole operation. She told him where to go to sell, and how much to sell. She made sure he did just what he was told to do. It seemed as though she was manipulating him. I started to bring my grades up in school. Then I found out that I had some major school fees that needed to be paid before graduation. I wasn't really worried because of all the money that was coming in I knew I would be able to get it from my mother. When I went to my mother with the bills, she flat out told me she didn't have the money. I truly found this hard to believe, because from dusk to dawn they would stay out all hours of the day selling drugs. *So how the fuck could she tell me she didn't have the money?* Apparently my mother's boyfriend wasn't doing right with the money, and they had to keep selling to pay back the loan they received from their distributor. So I had no way of paying off the loans I owed for school. My mother's boyfriend entered my room, and told me the only way I could make up this money was if I worked for it. *Well no shit Sherlock!* I couldn't find a job that would pay me what I needed, plus I refused to work and support their grown asses - while they sold drugs. He got up, closed my door, and came back to sit on my bed. Now, at this point with all the shit I'd experienced, I knew where this was leading; and I hoped and prayed that he wouldn't go there with me *(Especially because he definitely was not cute).* He said, *"I know a quick way for you to make some money, and you only need to do it for a couple of hours."* In my head I thought...

A COUPLE OF HOURS, YOU DAMN FREAK....but I didn't say it out loud. He pulled out this bag that had hundreds of little baggies inside it. When I saw them, I knew exactly what he wanted me to do. He told me if I worked the 12am to 4am shift on the corner, he would give me $300. Yes, he wanted me to sell some crack for him. Inside, I knew that from this moment on, he wasn't a real man. I mean yes I was eighteen years old, but I was still in high school with a bright future ahead of me. He was asking me to risk all of that, just so he could get a good night's sleep. What kind of man would allow his girlfriend's son to risk being robbed, killed, raped or thrown in jail. I wasn't really surprised, not at all, because these were the type of men my mother dealt with. I actually expected something like this to come from him much sooner. Well needless to say, I said yes. I needed the money desperately. I had no idea what I was getting myself into. He came outside with me for the first half hour to tell me the do's and the don'ts of selling drugs on the street.

Don't make eye contact.

Don't talk to them.

If they take too long then it's a set-up, and you need to run.

If they give you change beat their ass.

...and look out for police in unmarked cars.

I made mental notes of everything that he said. I still wasn't really paying attention due to the fact I was freezing. It was winter in Chicago, and I was freezing my ass off. Why were people out there buying crack in the middle of winter in the first damn place! I didn't care, I just needed to work for a couple of hours, get this money, so I could walk across the stage and receive my diploma. I wasn't far from my house, just a couple blocks, but far enough away so people didn't know where I lived. The action was very light; I couldn't wear ear phones - I had to stay alert at all times. So I began to hum a few tunes in my head. I don't remember exactly what I was humming at the time. I thought about my grandmother who had recently passed away. I bet she was turning over in her grave watching her family's lives unfold the way they had. I wasn't dressed for this weather...it would have been hard to run with too many clothes on you feel me!   A few customers started coming up to me, and I was selling bags left and right. A couple of people looked at me twice as if they recognized me. Some of them knew exactly where they knew me from. I sold my bags pretty quickly and I decided to walk home, since I had nothing else to do. As I walked home I heard noises from around the way. As I walked back to my house I was still in shock over what I had just done...I, Cordaro, had sold crack cocaine on the mean streets of Chicago, IL. I laughed aloud because I couldn't believe what I just said. I wasn't cut out for this kind of life. I was a fat sissy and if someone tried to rob me, I would have given them everything I had without hesitation. My life was way more important than $300......

This couldn't be my life.

I knew my destiny.

I knew what I wanted to do with my life.

....being a side piece to a down low man and selling crack wasn't it.

I walked home and saw my mother's boyfriend outside our house selling to some crack heads. Why the hell was he selling this stuff out of our home where we lived, ate, and slept? This was supposed to be our safe haven. This man was simply destroying our entire lives, and he didn't seem to care. I didn't see this ending well at all. As I walked past him, he asked me how much money I made. I told him how much I had made and how many bags I had sold. He told me to keep the money, and just give him the supply I had left. As I handed him the supply, I noticed an unmarked car driving very slowly past our house. I didn't pay it much attention, then I remembered what he told me about unmarked cars - that meant police activity. Immediately, I got scared and ran into the house to my mother who was in the kitchen. As I ran into the kitchen I saw her and some of her friends counting money and stashing some drugs in empty cereal boxes. I told my mother what I saw and everyone went into high alert. She turned off the kitchen lights and looked out the back window and saw footprints in the snow. Her boyfriend came in, slammed the front door and told us we were about to be raided. My mother took the stash out of my hand and flushed it down the toilet. Everyone ran around like crazy people screaming *"go!"*, *"hide..."* Then I heard a loud *BANG!* What the hell was that? We all nearly jumped out of our skin....we didn't know where the noise came from. I was terrified, so I ran into the front room and sat on the loveseat in the corner. *BANG! BANG!* I heard two more of these sounds more clearly now this time. We had three doors that led to the inside of our home, a screen door, a front porch door and the door for the living room. *It all made sense now……* **THE POLICE ARE BURSTING THROUGH MY HOUSE!** I instantly thought about my sister and jumped off the couch, ran to her room when the last sound occurred….*BANG!* A smoke bomb was tossed two inches from my feet. I fell to my knees and started screaming for my mother's help. I heard her scream from the kitchen, but she couldn't get to me. My eyes were closed the whole time, because of the smoke. When I finally opened my eyes, two black objects stared me in the face. I realized these were guns pointing at my face. *"Get down on the ground, get your fat ass on the ground!"* These were the words that the policeman were constantly yelling at from behind their weapons. They didn't touch me, they just kept yelling at me asking me the same question.

"Where is he?

"Where is he?"

I didn't know who they were talking about. Then I heard three gun shots. I screamed my mother's name to make sure she was okay, but she didn't respond. *"Noooooooooo" was all I heard* coming from the direction of the kitchen. It was my mother's voice. I exhaled. At least I knew my mother was not hurt….even though I was still terrified to find out who actually had been hurt. My mother was brought to the front of the house where I was, and when I saw her, I wanted to jump up and hug her. My mother looked embarrassed. She was crying, and I could tell she couldn't believe that this was happening to us. The house that she and her children were raised in had been destroyed. She was forced to watch as her son, (who was being pinned down with a gun in his face) tremble with fear. I'm sure in that moment, she was seconds away from throwing in the towel and giving up. It turned out that the police officers were only looking for my mother's boyfriend. An undercover agent had caught him selling drugs right on our front porch. They didn't have a warrant for anyone else in the house or to search our property. They only had a warrant to seize his property and arrest him. How stupid could he be to sell drugs out of our house? I knew this piece of shit was going to destroy my family one day. *Why the fuck didn't my mother listen to me?* No dick has ever been that good, that I would risk losing my entire family over. If this had happened today, I'm sure that I would have been shot as they raided the house. I could have would have been another *hashtag* of this generation. The police officers arrested him right in front of us all. This drama was too much to handle and to see my little sister in the middle of it, made it even more emotional. I had to go outside and cool off. As I walked outside I saw my two dogs were lying shot to death in the snow. Instantly I fell to my knees in tears.

I didn't know what to do.

I couldn't face my mother after that. I was so disappointed in her and the life decisions she had made. Not only did they affect her, but they affected my sister and I as well.

I was tired...plain and simple. Tired of being the adult and taking care of everyone. This just became too much for me to handle and I needed a way out. If the cops had shown up thirty minutes earlier, they would have caught me selling bags crack and my life would have been ruined forever. After the raid, a lot of things changed for me and my family. We were kicked out of our home by the (village), and were forced to move out in a week. The home I grew up in was boarded up as if meant nothing. All of our memories were destroyed. There was no way for us to take everything we owned in a week. So unfortunately, we had to leave some things behind. My mother decided that while her boyfriend was in jail, she needed to get her life back on track. In order to do that, she decided to move into a shelter in Minnesota. This was a shelter for battered women and if she finished the program, they would get her an apartment and help her to get back on her feet. *That was the one thing I admired about my mother.* She knew how to get back up after life knocked down. She was going to provide for her children....by any means necessary. This time, I was left out of the picture. Even though I was only eighteen years old and I was still in my last semester of high school; I was considered an adult. So I couldn't go with my mother to Minnesota. Leaving me behind was one of the hardest things I think my mother ever had to do. I know she felt as though she had failed me. *I didn't see it that way.* I felt as though this was my path. For some reason, God was going to bring me through this, and I would emerge victorious. Yes, I was still very spiritual, even after everything I had gone through. I was pissed at God for so long. I felt he was ignoring my cries for help. So I turned to all I knew at the time.

Men.

I actually began to take pleasure in being the *fuck boy* for men. I was basically homeless living with family members that claimed they would support me while my mother was away. *They lied!* I was supporting myself, I would do what I knew would get me some quick money. I started turning tricks with my best friend's boyfriend. He would set up some guys who he knew were on the down low, and wanted to have fun. I would show them a good time for money. He wouldn't let me have sex with them that in his mind, was taking things too far. If they wanted their dick sucked, or to eat my ass; or simply to fuck my throat - it didn't matter as long as they paid. There were various types of men, but a lot of them were thugs - guys who you wouldn't normally think would be gay. This would become my *"type"*. No one really knew this not even my best friend, who eventually stopped talking to me. I believe the truth finally set in after a few years. *He didn't want her. He was still messing around with me.*

 At this point all I wanted to do was survive, so losing her friendship to make sure I had some cash in my pocket was okay with me. A person reaches a point in their life, when everything turns into an *out-of- body experience*. I would sit and watch myself allow these men use and mistreat me, and I didn't think there was anything wrong with it.

I mean all the men in my life.

We were charging fifty dollars for an hour and we would split the money. Sometimes he tried to play me, and only give me ten, but I really didn't care I just wanted some money for lunch at school. I was still pushing forward with school and I was determined to finish on time. I will admit, I liked a lot of the guys I would hook up with. They had nice bodies, nice dicks...the works! They didn't want me to talk and they kept their eyes closed most of the time when I was giving them oral. I would never let them cum in my mouth, because to me, that was disrespect. I would get an extra thirty dollars under the table if I let them cum on my face. I would always accept that *Chanel* good moisturizer. My father didn't do anything to help me while I was going through this tough time. Eventually he offered me a place to sleep at a house he was barely allowed to stay in. I had no support from my uncles, mentors or my pastor. I was at my lowest and had to find a way to pull myself out of this rut, or the next stop for my life was a cemetery.

My body was tired.

I was physically exhausted.

I decided enough was enough.

I could no longer live my life this way.

After I graduated from high school, I tried a lot of trade schools and community colleges, but I needed to be on a campus. *It was the only way to know I had a secure place to sleep at night and a guaranteed meal.* My grades were good enough to get me into college. *But which one?* While applying for colleges, I still spoke with my mother on a regular basis. She had successfully graduated from her program, and she had an apartment. She was still under watch, and had rules to abide by, but she is back on her own and that feeling was amazing to me. She wanted so badly to sneak me into her apartment. I didn't want her risk getting caught and having to start all over somewhere else... I slowed down on communicating to the guy I stole from my best friend, and focused on bettering myself. I moved in with a cousin, *(who also had a terrible upbringing)* so she knew and understood my struggle. Everything seemed to be going well, I had a job, and I was focused on me. There wasn't a down low man in sight.

Or so I thought! I don't know why I couldn't get rid of their asses!

I was living in a house with a cousin, who would fuck her boyfriend every single night! He came down to the basement one night and wakes me from my sleep. The combinations of her snores and my moans, would have made a fucked up *R&B* song. There was something different about his sex. He had that grown man sex thing going on. All this time, I thought the guy I had been messing around with, had the biggest dick ever...but his dick wasn't shit compared to this grown ass man. There is nothing like a man that knows exactly what he wants, and doesn't have to wait for it. He didn't play around with his feelings. From the first moment he made a pass at me, he told me this was just going to be a fuck thing and nothing more. When he told me this, I was prepared to protect my heart and not get attached to him. Older mature men have a goal in mind when they fuck, and that is to fuck you so right; that you can't function or think of anyone else. Older men get more pleasure knowing that what they are doing is pleasing you and making you happy. His presence alone made me do whatever he told me. One night when I was bent over, he started eating my ass getting it nice and wet and stroking his dick at the same time. I was so ready for what was about to come next. I started taking all nine inches of that fat dick, and then I saw a letter from *Alabama A&M University* laying on my bed. I didn't think anything of it, because I hadn't heard back from any other colleges by that time. I just knew I didn't get in. He flipped me over and fucked me on my back. Now this position was tough, because he pinned my knees so I couldn't move. I felt every inch of him moving in and out of my tight ass while in this position. Older men like fucking slow, so they feel every moment of your ass creaming on their dicks. I wasn't in much pain, because again, he was a grown man; and he prepared me for this. He wanted me to enjoy this just as much as he did. I was definitely enjoying every minute of it, but I had to open this damn letter. He was cuming, I could feel it because his dick started throbbing, and he started pumping me faster. My moans grew much louder to the point I didn't give a fuck if she heard me. My body shook as I opened the letter. I couldn't focus on him or getting myself off, because the letter was more important to me at time. I almost cried, as I read the most encouraging words ever written….. *CONGRATULATIONS, YOU HAVE BEEN ACCEPTED.*

The End….For Now!

About the Author

I am so happy you have read this book. This book is not just for the LGBT Community or the black community, this book is for all that have given themselves to someone and have not felt the love in return. I started writing this book 2011 when it was going to be a play. As I was writing the play it just became more and more difficult to follow the storyline, so I decided that the story would make a great book. I hope you believe that it's a great book as well. I dedicate this book to the families and survivors of the PULSE Nightclub shooting. That incident made me realize that life is what you make of it and we must keep pushing for the generation of LGBT fighters who haven't come yet.